Time in Passing

ISBN-13:
978-0692983294 (Victoria Jenkins)

ISBN-10:
0692983295

First Printing, 2017

Contents

Past

Wrong

There was a time when I didn't believe
I could ever write this.

Here I am, proving
Myself wrong, and hopefully providing
Inspiration for you.

Thinking About Mistakes

I constantly consider everything
I could've done
To make you stay.

I'm living in the present
While my mind is in the past.

I need to try to think in the future.

You're so Forgetful

You wish to forget what we had but
I wish to remember the epic tale we told
With our tongues
Whispering words in each other's ears,
Happy and joyously inseparable.
You can't just forget it,
Can you?

Unfixable

My heart has been shattered
Only once.

The other lovers said
Here, have mine
Giving me an
Already broken heart
Just to shatter
To an atomic size.

Was

Looking back on it I realize how
Blinded I was by the
Rose-colored glasses
Of false security and
Fake admiration.
Oh what a mess
It was.

Of Success

You tried to pull me out of the
Darkness I was encapsulated in.

All you did was blind me
With the bright lights.

Enlightened

The keys of the piano
Ring in my mind.
Your fingers caressing the keys
Creating a sweet serenade
As soft as my voice as it joined in
Singing higher
Up in the clouds and
Away from this judgemental world
That shatters the dreams of the
used-to-be dreamers
And want-to-be lovers.
We called this
A way to pass the time
Until the day came
When your fingers no longer played
Those black and white keys for me
And my voice no longer sang
Those tear jerking notes for you.

He Stared

As if she was the most
Beautiful thing in the world.

Because there were still other
Beautiful things and she wasn't his only everything.

He was playing with
The idea.

Always In Your Memories

Why do you regret ever
Being a part of my life?
In the end it was good.

You made me a better person,
And opened my eyes to what a
Real man is not.

Secrets Shared

So all along it was you
Sitting in the corner writing
Realms and realms of
Hangovers and cigarettes
Whilst sipping a strong, black
Coffee with skim milk and
One sugar. I thought I knew
You but all I know is how to
Make a bad coffee.

This Is For You

I've thought about walking up to you
Uttering the two words I
Practiced over and over.
Too bad;
I have a greater sense of self worth
So I believe
I am deserving of much more
Than the three words
Crudely scribbled and wildly crossed out
On the inside of a book
That told me I was independent
Strong
Beautiful
And worthy of so much more than
A phrase that meant nothing on the tongue
Of a liar.

I hope you read these poems and realize
You lost so much more
Than you ever believed.

Plastic Surgery

People's opinions don't physically change you
In any way.
Why should they affect you mentally?
I'm glad I don't let society
Tell me what's right and wrong anymore.

Pottery

The hardships of the past
Shaped my heart and hands
Into dry clay spheres:

Unlovable,
Circular,
Untouchable.

Zinnia

You tended to her because at the time
She was the
Most beautiful.

Too bad she was an annual,
Blooming only once:
An unfortunate fad.

Shattered Reflections

Our reflections in the dirty mirror lied to us.
What we saw was the impeccable fantasy
We wished for ourselves.

We wouldn't ever live out this fantasy;
We'd have to let our alternate universe selves expe-
rience it.

Can We Ever Be More?

It was that evening
On the hill made of our childhood memories
That I first noticed the way

I loved you was not
Just friends

I realized it too late
In a haze of broken glass
And an unbreakable pact

Between a best friend
And a person who was late to everything.

Gunshots Rang Out

The world was pure;
Their intentions were dark.
The two contrasted like
White walls
covered with the red splatters
Of the insantiy
Of the inhumane humanity.

A Warning I Ignored

You yelled so loud
The world shook in fear.

It knew what was wrong
And worried I didn't.

Present

What a Wreck

It's a terrifying thought
That I have constantly.
I think about my thoughts;
How nobody knows them.
My unspoken ideas and sentences
That will never be recorded.

All I can do is hope my
Chopped up sentences stacked upon one another
Are enough to help you understand;
My messy mind.

New World

Newborns are blind
To the horrors of the world
Until they open their eye for the first time
And scream in fear,
Seeing where they will waste their time.

Universal Symbols

Words are overused
Overcomplicated,
And overthought.

Actions are in.

Smiles exchanged by strangers are
The simplest ways of saying
All the words too beautiful for our minds to under-
stand.

There was a hot evening when we stayed up. Listening to your perfectly curated playlist, discussing. Things that could never be discussed in daylight. I think this is when I realized you were my best friend. And this would never change. Discordant with my other distant friends that drift in and out like my thoughts when I'm sitting in a cafe staring at the rain. Pitter patter on the window and there you are, climbing through it and into my room. So different we are at night when everything is real and you feel alive and the moon is out. Shining like the stars on the silver screen smiling and sneaking down the stairs. Eating strawberries because what good is going out if we have each other? And I swear those strawberries were so terrible but it didn't matter because we were laughing. Sweet laughs to sweeten the rotten strawberries of the awkward years. There is no greater feeling in the world than laying on the floor at 3:30am knowing that in 3 hours you have to be looking. Even though the lack of sleep leaves you feeling dead, the opposite of how you feel with them: a makeup-free tangled-hair un-shaven-legs wreck that has never been more human before. We are so wildly different during day until the moon rises along with our emotions bubbling inside of us as we share more and more until we fall asleep on the floor while the timeless playlist plays on. The backdrop to a wild friendship that will only get more and more beautiful as time goes on. How else can I say this?

A Time In-Between

There are people that never fail to encapsulate me in their oceans of stories. From the time in-between our visits; our short storytelling. Text messages don't do us justice. We share through gigantic hand gestures followed by loud yelling full of joy and passion ending when we can't breathe anymore, clutching our lungs. Those moments of silence in-between the extra accentuated stories. Then we run away on separate paths to experience the upcoming stories we will share the next time our paths cross.

Dreams Of The Future

I would've never guessed I'd
Be up past my nonexistent
Bedtime with my phone pressed against my face.

Whispers of stories of cities you've dreamed of vis-
iting with me
Falling from my lips to my pillowcase.

Infinite Infinities

We sit here for
What feels like an infinity.

Eventually that infinity becomes a
Piece of the past and a memory of another memory
In less than an infinity.

People say that before you die your life flashes be-
fore your eyes.
Well then why did your gaze from across the room
Instantly rewind a well scripted movie
Of my life
Featuring you?

Things Changed

I used to come home with
A smile on my face and
A story to tell
About a game on the playground.

Now I come home with
A tired face
A mouth to be kept shut and
A story untold.

The Only Reasons

Why are you alive
In this moment?
How are you changing the world
In this moment?

Somebody will be kissing you
Because you lived through this moment.
Somebody will be missing you
Because you lived through this moment.

A Friendly Face

I write these poems
In the late hours of the night
To keep me company
When I can't be alone any longer.

It's All In My Head

Poems fill my mind.
I try to avoid thinking about
Your disgustingly delightful face.
It doesn't work;
My mind writes poems about you, my hands
Transcribe them.

Words With Friends

I shouldn't be doing this
It's so wrong but so right.

Then don't do it.

I'll never be able to look in the mirror again
Knowing I let you get away.

Comfortable Dwellings

I dwell in my head
Alone and comfortable
Away from the noise
Commotion
My perfect universe
Where anything can
Happen until I have to
Face the reality of
Life and
truth.

Noise Cancelling

There's a small voice
In my head
Telling me
Stop.

To bad it wasn't loud enough
To drown out my determination
To carry on.

Pest Control

I need you now
To save me from my thoughts
And to help me stand back up
Wipe the tears off my face
Brush my hair
And exterminate the spiders nesting in my soul.

You'll Get the Hang of it Sooner or Later

It's her first day and you can tell
She's lost.

Just there, trying to hold on to the ropes
Like the businessmen holding their hands in tightly
clenched fists,
Waiting fervently for their morning doses of caf-
feine.
Her hands shake, spilling the coffee over the sides
of cups,
Her voice shakes, quavering while she calls out
names unsurely.

She'll get the hang of it,
There's still a chance.

Noticing Things

You think they don't see
Any of the madness in the world
but let me tell you, they notice
The way their fathers yell
While drinking that murky brown brew
and the way their mothers
work hours and hours and come home
late in the night wearing
clothes that smell like somebody else's home.
Trust me, they seem young but
they're aware of your whereabouts.

Running Out Of Oxygen

Isn't it strange that even though we're
Probably never going to talk again
I still go out of my way
Out of my comfort zone
To try and see you
To find your comforting presence in the sea
Of anxiety I'm drowning in.

Time Travel

I thought that without you
Life would be easier.

I wish I could go back and convince myself
That I was enough and that you
Really did love me more.

Future

A Better Tomorrow?

I worry that my future
Is not going to
Play out the way it does
In my head.

How can I live in a city
Where there is only
Hate and terror;
No hope?

The Liar And The Author

I only saved your number because
I made a promise to give you a copy
Of the topic of our boring conversations.

I unfollowed your social media but
Didn't block you because maybe someday
I'd be older and you'd not be a liar.

I wake up every morning and tell myself
Don't text him.
I think this is best for me and for you.

It Blew Over And Left Us

It looks like it might rain
Sometime later today.

I hope it pours and washes away
The sins of the world.

I hope it rains so I can look up to sky and fill my
eyes
With raindrops of pure water
Untouched by the dirty hands of man.

Maybe the world will flood and
We will all become stories never told.

Maybe the storm will blow over.

We Have to Make it Happen

We can only dream of the days we'll spend
Traipsing through the
Wondrous arrays of fine French scarves and
Eating croissants in the small corner shop bakeries
With the waiter that knows just how to make every-
one feel
At ease and
At home.

We Hope

The birth of the earth
Was a happy day.

It gave us the hope of a future.

To-Do List

Something should go here
I'll write it tomorrow
When I forget the words I wanted
To say.

The Art of the Deal

The blinds are broken.
The string snapped because somebody
Pulled too hard on it
Like they were desperate to see the light
Breathe the fuliginous air of outside
Rich with toxins,
Killing us slowly.
And somehow, with all the signs under their stuffy
snotty noses
They don't believe it's happening.
They'll be drowning in the melted ice caps and
claim
Oh it's just a flash flood
Even though it happened over the course of
Decades, not in a flash.
This is not just another deal
This is the future of our earth
This is a determining decision of whether or not the
wretched human race
Will live on, only to destroy more worlds.

I Had My Reasons

Maybe someday I'll tell you all of the
Reasons why and all of the issues
And everything I was feeling.

Maybe when I figure them out
I'll give you a call,
Tell you why I left.

Keep Your Gaze Ahead

Words are therapy
I got happier as I wrote
About my emotions and experiences.

I don't look back on sad times
Often because all I can do
Is carry on living.

fin.

A huge thank-you to the following backers:

Claire Perez
Derek Jenkins
Elaine Jenkins
Jillian Payne
Joseph Gibbs
Matthew Barry
Sébastien Limbourg

Without your kind pledges on my Kickstarter campaign this book would not have been possible.

A special thank-you:

To mom, without your endless, loving support for all my crazy creative ideas I would've never become the person I am today.

To dad, without your endless supply of crazy creative ideas, I would've never thought about what I could do in life out of the ordinary.

To grandmommy, for editing so many essays and teaching me how to use words to express the stories you want to tell.

To grandaddy, for showing me the importance of books, chess, and politics.

To nanny and grandpa, for always taking the time to read my work and teach me how to make proper english tea, the only thing that kept me awake to write this book.

To grandpa goldfish, for always being there, and for showing me how important family is.

To Jonathan, for listening to me read you poems at 3 am on Saturday nights over the phone. Paris is going to happen, trust me!

To Jillian, for always having my back since the fourth grade. I don't know where I'd be today without a friend like you.

To Josh, the crazy twin who I couldn't live without. And to Ruby, the first person to ever read my poems, the only other person I know who enjoys listening to Ed Sheeran while making cupcakes at 2 in the morning.

I love you all to Paris and back.

Who are you?

Victoria Jenkins is a young woman growing up in West Palm Beach, Florida. Despite her "teenagery" look, she is well spoken as both a student and an author. From a young age Victoria was always enthralled in a book, reading under the covers past her bedtime with a flashlight. Now, she's writing poems in the margins of her notes during class, or reading under the covers past her undefined-bed-time with an iPhone flashlight. She is always politically active and voices her opinion, sometimes using her poems as a microphone, sometimes using her voice during class. Victoria is working her way through high school, aiming to graduate with an IB Diploma. She then hopes to attend a university in London, England. Coffee enthusiast and avid explorer, you can typically find Victoria sitting in a cafe thousands of miles from home, sipping an artisan latte and writing poems in a nearly-full notebook.

Read more of Victoria's work on theshorthair.com

www.ingramcontent.com/pod-product-compliance
Lightning Source LLC
Chambersburg PA
CBHW071103040426
42443CB00013B/3393